Contents

Food Memories

What is your favourite meal? Are you learning to cook? Do some foods remind you of a special occasion?

Today we can eat a wide variety of food from all around the world. Some foods are sold as prepared meals and are ready to put in the oven or microwave. It hasn't always been like this.

This photo of a Welsh grocer's shop was taken in 1969. Compare the choice of fruit and vegetables with what you can buy in supermarkets and shops today.

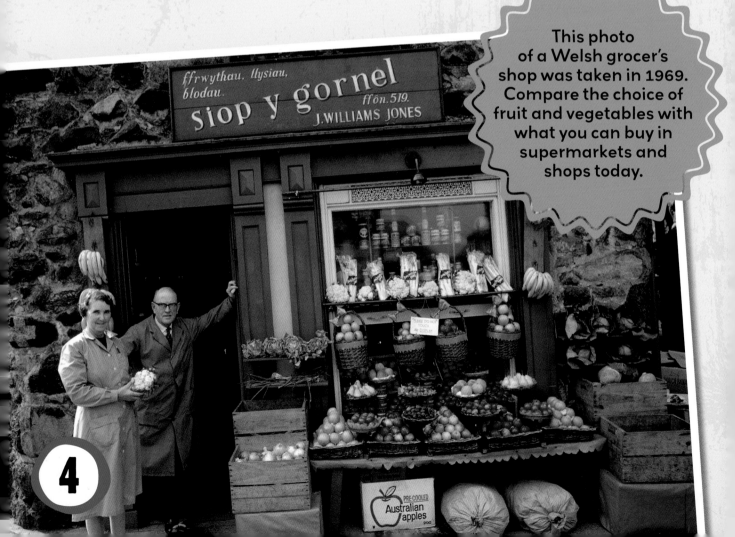

ffrwythau, llysiau, blodau.

siop y gornel

ffôn. 519.

J. WILLIAMS JONES

PRE-COOLED Australian apples

Tell ME What YOU Remember

FOOD

Sarah Ridley

W
FRANKLIN WATTS
LONDON • SYDNEY

Franklin Watts
Published in paperback in Great Britain in
2019 by The Watts Publishing Group

Series editor: Sarah Peutrill
Series design: Basement68

The Author and Publisher would
like to thank everyone who has
kindly contributed their photos
and memories to this book.

Dewey classification: 394.1'2'0941'0904
ISBN: 978 1 4451 4366 8
Library Ebook ISBN: 978 1 4451 4005 6

Printed in China

Franklin Watts
An imprint of
Hachette Children's Group
Part of The Watts Publishing Group
Carmelite House
50 Victoria Embankment
London EC4Y 0DZ

An Hachette UK Company
www.hachette.co.uk

www.franklinwatts.co.uk

Memories are what we remember about the past. People often have strong memories linked to food. Talking to people about what they remember can help us to learn about the past.

PURE BUTTER

Nick, born 1937, remembers...

Out shopping with my mother, we went from shop to shop to buy what we needed. At the grocer's, he cut off a slab of butter or a chunk of cheese, weighed it and wrapped it in paper. Some shops delivered food to our home.

Paul, born 1970, remembers...

This was my fourth birthday party. My mum held parties at home for me every year and always made the food herself. I loved the yellow jumper and wore it a lot.

Family Meals

People who grew up in the 1940s and 1950s remember sitting around a table for home-cooked family meals. This continued in many homes through the 1960s and 1970s, with some people using fish fingers or instant potato to save time. Then the TV dinner became popular. Does your family eat together at the end of the day?

Irene, born 1939, remembers...

My mum was a good cook. She'd do a roast on Sunday and then you'd have it minced on Monday. They were always tasty roast dinners, with gravy and Yorkshire puddings. We always sat down for meals, like this family.

Funda, born 1968, remembers...

We always ate as a family around the table when I was growing up. We are Cypriot so my mum cooked a mixture of Turkish and British dishes. We ate a lot of hummus, pitta bread, olives, grilled halloumi and koftes long before they became popular with everybody else.

When this photo was taken in 1989, the children were eating around the table while their parents carried on with the cooking.

FIND OUT MORE

Charis, born 2004, remembers...

During the week, my dad never eats with us as he is still at work. Our meals have to fit around what else we are doing, like going to clubs. Sometimes we have a bowl of cereal at bedtime if we are hungry.

Ask your parents and grandparents about their memories of family meals.

7

Wartime Rationing

When the Second World War broke out in 1939, British people were used to eating food grown abroad and brought to Britain by ship. Soon enemy submarines were sinking these ships, so shops started to run out of certain foods. To share out the food that was available, the government introduced rationing and gave everyone a ration book.

Roger, born 1940, remembers...

The shopkeeper stamped the coupons inside the ration book and my mother handed over the correct money. She was only allowed to buy small amounts of rationed foods. She made a wonderful bacon and onion roll with our bacon ration.

Food rationing started in 1940 with the rationing of butter, sugar and bacon. Bread was not rationed until 1946. Food rationing stopped in 1954.

Long queues formed outside food shops during the war. The fruit and vegetables sold by this greengrocer were never rationed but often ran out. How much did cabbages cost on the day this photo was taken?

Barbara, born 1932, remembers...

I remember eating a lot of carrots. We grew them in our vegetable plot. We were told that RAF pilots ate carrots to help them see in the dark.

DOCTOR CARROT
the Children's best friend
VIT-A

FIND OUT MORE

'Doctor Carrot' appeared on posters and leaflets to encourage people to eat more carrots. Find out about 'Potato Pete'.

Dig for Victory

During the Second World War, the British needed to grow more food. While farmers ploughed up meadows, people dug up their lawns and planted vegetables. Some people grew vegetables on new allotments in parks, schools or football grounds.

Barbara, born 1932, remembers...

We grew potatoes, carrots, rhubarb, raspberries, gooseberries and blackcurrants. We kept a few hens at a farm nearby. My mum helped to look after the garden and made blackcurrant jam that we used to make a hot drink in the winter.

Joe, born 1935, remembers...

People belonged to pig clubs down at the local allotments. They shared the cost of buying the pig and used food waste to fatten it up. We put our food waste in the collecting bin on our street.

These London children were living in Wales to keep them safe from air raids. Children helped to harvest crops in the countryside. Farmers needed their help because many farm workers were fighting in the forces.

FIND OUT MORE

Find some recipes dating from the Second World War and try them out.

Shopping for Food

How does your family shop for food? From the 1930s to the 1960s most people went shopping every day, picking up fresh foods from different shops or markets. In the 1950s the first supermarkets opened. Since then, they have grown bigger and bigger and sell almost everything.

1950s

Joan, born 1932, remembers...

I served behind the dry goods counter in a Sainsbury's store in the 1940s and 1950s. I knew all m[y] customers. They had to move fro[m] counter to counter, queueing each time to buy bacon, then cheese, tea or sugar.

Joan, born 1932, remembers...

1970s

I stopped work when I had my son in 1957. Gradually all the Sainsbury's stores became self-service, which we didn't like at first. It was quicker to walk around with a wire basket and pay for goods at the end but it was much less friendly.

Funda, born 1968, remembers...

1968

My parents were born in Cyprus but moved to London before I was born. Mum and Dad shopped at the local Cypriot shops. Supermarkets did not sell the same range of foods we can buy today.

FIND OUT MORE

Compare the photos of the two Sainsbury's stores.

13

Keeping Food Fresh

In the past, people had to go shopping almost every day because they did not own a fridge or a freezer to keep their food fresh. People stored food in the coldest part of the house. By the early 1970s many people owned a fridge and, 20 years later, most of them owned a freezer as well.

1920s Only a few families owned a fridge because they were very expensive.
1971 Seventy per cent of homes had a fridge.
Mid 1990s Most homes had a freezer.

Jessie, born 1940, remembers...

The larder was the coldest room in the house. My mum kept the cheese, butter and milk there, as well as the meat in the meat safe.

A meat safe

Jane, born 1963, remembers...

We had a fridge like the one in the advert but it never had this much food in it! It had a small icebox for ice cubes. My mum bought a chest freezer in the late 1970s and kept it in the garage.

No stowaways aboard.

Birds Eye Cod Fillet Fish Fingers have only 100% natural ingredients. No artificial colours or flavourings.

Jordan, born 1987, remembers...

We had a fridge freezer in the kitchen. Mum cooked us lots of frozen fish fingers, chicken nuggets and mini pizzas for tea. We liked the Captain Bird's Eye adverts on the TV.

FIND OUT MORE

Compare your fridge to the one shown in the Electrolux advert. What is the same and what is different?

15

In the Kitchen

Eighty years ago, many women were still cooking on a range. Fitted kitchens became popular from the 1950s onwards. Since then, many time-saving machines have become normal in people's kitchens, such as dishwashers, food processors and microwave ovens.

Jessie, born 1940, remembers...

My mother cooked on a range like this one when I was very little. When gas pipes were laid in the village, my parents bought a gas cooker for their new kitchen.

This advert for a fitted kitchen dates from 1955. Find the electric cooker, stainless steel sink and the fridge. The worktops were made from new materials that were easy to wipe clean.

English Rose Kitchen Equipment

Sarah, born 1973, remembers...

We got a new fitted kitchen in the early 1980s. Like the family in this photo (below), we ate all of our meals there. My mum was pleased with her dishwasher, double oven, fridge and freezer. Later she got a microwave.

Here is a photo of me peeping around the edge of the old cooker when it was being taken out.

FIND OUT MORE

Compare these kitchens, dating from 1946, 1955 and 1981. What is the same and what is different?

17

Learning To Cook

Who does the cooking at home?
In the past, most people learnt to cook from their own parents. From the 1950s onwards, cookery programmes on TV started to inspire people to try out different recipes. Today most children have cookery classes at secondary school.

Irene, born 1939, remembers...

My mother had a Be-Ro cookbook and I still use a sponge cake recipe from it. Be-Ro made flour and gave away free recipe books. In the 1970s I lived in Leicester where there was a big Indian community. I started cooking chicken curries using leftover chicken, apples and sultanas.

Delia Smith was one of the first TV cooks to become really famous. This photo was taken when she had her first TV cookery programme in 1973. Her cookbooks taught people to cook.

Simon, born 1963, remembers...

Like this boy, I learnt how to cook a few things in school cookery classes. My pineapple upside-down cake went down well at home.

Meera, born 1980, remembers...

My mother learnt to cook from her mother so we ate the same meals as she had eaten when she was growing up in India, with a few different ingredients.

FIND OUT MORE

How did people in your family learn to cook – at school, at home or not at all?

Changing Tastes

In the 1950s and 1960s more and more people could afford to go on holiday abroad and eat out in restaurants. They tasted different foods and wanted to cook them at home. Also at this time, many people from Commonwealth countries and elsewhere were making new homes for themselves in Britain.

This Caribbean family were photographed in their Birmingham kitchen in 1965. As more people settled in Britain, shops and market stalls started to sell a much wider choice of spices, vegetables, fruits and dry goods.

In the 1980s, on my first holiday abroad, we went to Greece. I was excited about trying this fancy ice cream with a sparkler but sadly I didn't like the taste as it was made from goats' milk! Greek food was quite unusual then but now it's available everywhere and I love it.

In the 1950s there were six Indian restaurants in Britain but 50 years later there were over 8,000. Today people eat Indian food regularly, at home (often from 'ready meals') or in restaurants.

FIND OUT MORE

Ask your grandparents when they first ate at an Indian or Chinese restaurant.

Sweets

Ask adults you know about the sweets they enjoyed when they were young. These words might jog their memories: blackjacks, liquorice, gobstoppers, Spangles, Opal Fruits, Love Hearts, jelly beans and Haribo.

Roger, born 1940, remembers...

I used my pocket money and my ration coupons to buy wine gums and other sweets from the corner shop. I dipped a liquorice stick into a packet of sherbet and licked the sherbet off it.

During the Second World War, childre. had to make their small sweet ration last a week. When rationing ended in 1953, these children rushed into a shop to buy their favourite lollipops.

Timeline

Use this timeline to see at a glance some of the information in this book.

1930s–1940s People had to shop every day as few owned fridges. When shopping, they walked from shop to shop buying meat from the butcher, fruit and vegetables from the greengrocer, dry goods and cheese from the grocer and so on. Many shops offered to deliver food shopping to people's homes by van or delivery bike.

1940–1954 Food rationing was brought in during and after the Second World War (1939–1945).

1950s The first supermarkets opened. Fitted kitchens became popular. More and more people settled in Britain, bringing their own national dishes to Britain. According to the British Library, there were six Indian restaurants in Britain.

1955 Bird's Eye sold the first frozen fish fingers.

1971 Seventy per cent of homes had a fridge.

1973 onwards Delia Smith appeared in the first of many TV cookery programmes.

1980s–1990s More pre-prepared meals available to buy.

Mid 1990s Most homes had a freezer.

2004 According to the British Library, there were over 8,000 Indian restaurants in Britain.

2014 Cookery lessons had to be taught in all schools.

Glossary

Allotment A small plot of land for growing vegetables and fruit.

Commonwealth The Commonwealth is a group of 53 countries, most of which were once ruled by Britain.

Counter In a shop, the long flat surface or display cabinet at which the customer is served.

Dry goods Food that is solid and dry, such as flour, tea or sugar.

Greengrocer Someone who runs a shop which sells fruit and vegetables.

Grocer Someone who runs a shop which sells mostly food, but usually not fruit and vegetables.

Halloumi A cheese made in Cyprus from goats' or sheeps' milk.

Kofte Grilled lamb meatballs, originally from Turkey.

Meat safe A wooden box with wire mesh in the door, for keeping meat away from flies or pets.

RAF This stands for Royal Air Force, Britain's air force, formed during the First World War (1914–1918).

Range A cooking stove, usually fuelled by coal, which often heated the water for the home as well.

Ration book A book containing coupons that were cut out or stamped by a shopkeeper when someone wanted to buy rationed goods.

Second World War The world war that took place between 1939 and 1945.

Sweet ration The sweet ration varied during the war but was often just one small bar of chocolate or a small bag of sweets per week.

TV dinners The name for all types of ready meals, such as pizzas, pasta bakes and chicken tikka, that have been pre-cooked and only need to be reheated and served.

Index